PRAISE FOR PETER SCHMITT

"Peter Schmitt presents a compelling, responsible, deeply felt and even exalted imagination that knows its way about the various worlds of immediacy, memory, dream, or fantasy, that we all inhabit in one way or another. His range is exemplary and, most persuasively of all, his poems are altogether without pretensions, as if they had been smelted down to draw off any possible impurities. They exhibit, in consequence, the ring of integrity so rare that it deserves the honor of our delight and gratitude."

> - Anthony Hecht, Pulitzer Prize-winning poet

"Peter Schmitt is a kind of poet I particularly admire, a kind lately too much in the minority: one who writes lucid poems in precise language about life as it is."

> - Donald Justice, Pulitzer Prize-winning poet

GOODBYE, APOSTROPHE

Peter Schmitt

Regal House Publishing

Published by
Regal House Publishing, LLC
Raleigh, NC 27612
All rights reserved

ISBN -13 (paperback): 9781646030545
ISBN -13 (epub): 9781646030460
Library of Congress Control Number: 2020930412

Interior and cover design by Lafayette & Greene
lafayetteandgreene.com
Cover images © by anna42f/Shutterstock

Regal House Publishing, LLC
https://regalhousepublishing.com

Printed in the United States of America

in loving memory
of my mother, Evelyn
(1925 – 2014)

Contents

I

THE SPRINTER

She ran track, was all I knew—a sprinter—
and wordless at the back seemed no more there

than on days away traveling with the team;
her poems predictable, perfunctory,

all false starts and pulling up too soon, never
exceeding the line minimum, skinny

on the page and always the single rushed draft,
as if writing were a race to finish

as fast as she could, subjects pedestrian,
tedious, forgettable, for her no doubt

as much as the reader. Until one day
late in the term, regionals looming, she dropped

on my desk three solid pages of long,
gripping lines, so much stronger than anything

she'd turned in before, as though the language
were compelled to rise to the occasion—

and did—relaying with heartstopped clarity
just what her father had been doing to her

for the past seven years—and how no one knew,
not even her mother… What I can't tell you,

of course, is that from that moment forward
her life changed—he met justice, she found freedom—

not because it didn't happen, but because
it wasn't for me to know, and I didn't.

And her writing the rest of that semester?
As you'd expect, never as expressive

again, nothing else summoning that force…
But the poem had opened something in her,

as she passed it to a coach, who notified
counselors…and she kept on competing, battling,

which is how I'll think of her: springing away
from her blocks, arms and legs churning, the head down,

then slowly coming up, as she'd been taught.

THE SKELETON IN MY GRANDFATHER'S CLOSET

hung in their bedroom
for years after he died,
my grandmother dutifully dusting
the yellowing life-size model
from his surgical days.
Who can say

if she ever let time settle
on the stack of letters
she found from the nurse—
but she took my father with her
(he was six) from Brooklyn
to Oakland on the *Zephyr*,

booking so late
every berth was reserved.
The nerve of that woman,
she might've muttered, and *How
could he bring them home?*
Unsure she'd bring herself

home, or their son.
Sleeping upright was no bargain
while he roamed the observation car,
a storm out over the Rockies
lighting up the glassed-in deck
like an x-ray.

By the time the Bay
washed into view, sun burning
through fog, she saw how it was,
and penned my grandfather a letter
of her own—one he saved
only he knew where—

because it saved him.

FAT KID

Three hundred pounds in seventh grade and growing,
fattest kid in school, Sid in the horn section
nearly blocked my view of our director
from where I labored, back row, on tenor sax.
I could see his neck going pink, sweat slipping
down Dizzy Gillespie cheeks, eyes squinting
as his stubby fingers worked the keys. We lived
two blocks apart. The bus ejected us
at the same stop: slight, skinny me, Big Sid.

That first week of school, we all saw it coming,
and when some tall, long-haired jerk shoved Sidney
in the dirt, a circle rapidly formed
and the coaches vanished like Darwinians
allowing natural selection to run
its course. All Sid could do was raise his fists,
but by then his glasses were broken, and he
was bleeding, and crying, and the crowd jeering.
Tears stung my eyes, but I let no one see them.

After that single, vicious beating, some kind
of equilibrium had been restored,
a necessary order imposed, which all
understood: Sid had to pay for his weight
with a pummeling, it was that simple.
And once endured, he earned a grudging respect;
his tormentor—now that he had filled his function
for us—meanwhile was relegated
to pariah, and dropped out in early Spring.

And so Sidney survived; the taunts continued,
but with lower volume, less frequency.
We learned our instruments, we rode the bus.
His mother, who might have outweighed her son,
kept to the cool back rooms of their dark house.
But she had to be glad to see him with friends,
even ones like me—as I would kid him too,
once in a while—and he would punch me,
hard, in the arm, because it wasn't all right,

and he'd make damned sure at least somebody knew.

WARTS AND ALL

"Devil follow corpse, cat follow devil, warts follow cat, I'm
done with ye!"
                        — Huck Finn, in *The Adventures of Tom Sawyer*

When we first meet Huck Finn, in *Tom Sawyer*,
he's swinging by the tail a dead cat—good,
he tells Tom, for curing warts—though you need
someone wicked just buried, and a devil
or two or three in the graveyard at midnight…

It sounds crazy to us now, like catching warts
from frogs, or Tom's remedy, spunk water—
rain that's pooled in a rotted-out stump—which Huck
refutes, by the way, citing as a source
a "nigger," whom even Tom must concede

likely wouldn't have lied, though he "never see
a nigger that *wouldn't*." That troublesome word
is all over *Tom Sawyer*, and of course
Huckleberry Finn, like the warts that sprouted
on my fingers when I was eleven,

those viral growths that festered along the nails
and their barely risen moons. Not long ago
a white publisher in Montgomery,
Alabama, tried to burn the word away
by changing it in his own printing of *Huck*

to the word "slave." It was hardly a salve.
He was like the dermatologist who dipped
a long cat-tailed Q-tip in a thermos
and swabbed my fingers with liquid nitrogen
so cold my hands were useless for an hour.

In days the warts blistered, fell off. And soon
came back. The word comes back. And which text whitewashed
next? *Tom Sawyer*, like the hero's famous fence,
the publisher's guilt liberally applied
like a coat of paint? It wasn't spunk water,

no, or burying bloodied beans, or even
a dead cat that finally cured my warts,
but in fact a cat very much alive—
our gray tabby Abigail, who took it
upon herself to lick my fingers for hours,

each day, after school for weeks, sandpaper tongue
persistent, methodical, slowly wearing
down the warts, until at last they disappeared,
not to return. And if it will happen,
it will happen that way—the word a wart

on everyone's hands, eventually erased
under everyone's rough tongue—leaving it
only in books, which, when we come across it
years from now, will send us to dictionaries,
and strike our ears as something harmless and quaint.

THE HANDS

On a ledge above the kitchen door
our mother set the plaster casts
of our hands—like little pies
left there to cool
we'd stuck all our fingers into.

First mine, then three years later
at the same kindergarten—
before he started going
to special schools—my brother's,
for a not-quite-matched set.

The doctors said he would never read.
But after school, our mother
quietly closed his door
and sat with him and an open book
for hours before she made dinner.

When frustration got the best of him
he'd run from the house,
slamming the kitchen door,
and the little blue plates
of our hands would waver, not wave.

They stayed up there for years,
where a horseshoe might have hung.
But it wasn't by luck
that he now reads.

When we moved, our mother held each hand

in her own, then stacked them in a box.

THE RIDE HOME

It was a mistake, probably, to give her
the ride home she asked for, approaching me

out of the night as I pumped gas—this woman
in her forties, in scuffed, hightop sneakers

and mullet haircut—and she must have sensed me
watching her from the corner of my eye,

waiting for the knife or the gun to flash,
to rob me or steal my car and leave me

by the side of the road. Even when I
bought her the Happy Meal at the drive-through

I kept expecting something to happen
as I followed her directions down streets

I'd never driven. She didn't talk about
what I would read, two years later, in the news:

the father whose plane disappeared somewhere
in the Bermuda Triangle; the mother

who wrestled professionally; her own stint
as an amateur boxer. Karate

black belt. Ninth-grade dropout, shrimpboat-mate, fifty-
story high-rise painter. The twenty-seven

arrests: drugs, prostitution, burglary.
No, she only went on about her daughter,

worried that the girl's new boyfriend couldn't be
trusted, she just had a feeling about him.

I wonder now if she told me these things
to put me at ease—*a caring mother*

wouldn't hurt you!—but I let out a breath
when we pulled up at last to the address

she called her own. She thanked me, then scribbled
on a receipt her name—*Sheila*—her number,

and said, "For plumbing, painting—I can do
almost anything." I never called it.

But I have time now to also wonder
if she approached him too, that final stranger,

at a gas station, and got him to buy her
some food, and told him about her daughter,

and only now does it occur to me
that maybe she was the one in my car

more scared—*you wouldn't hurt a caring mother?*
But I wasn't the one who veered off course

and left her corpse in a weed-choked vacant lot
between a body shop and the railroad tracks.

In the newspaper story about her death,
they've printed in color her likely mug shot:

hair cropped short, eyes heavy, she looks unhappy.
But a black and white from twenty years ago

shows her leaning back on a bench, hands taped,
toweling hair matted to her forehead,

yet pretty, and smiling, while a trainer
unlaces her ankle-high boxing shoes.

She could be fresh from a sparring session,
three tight rounds with the gym's most promising kid,

giving as she got, and thinking, *I can
do this. I can do almost anything.*

BOYHOOD: THE BURGLAR ALARM

The wooden bars of the burglar alarm
made an ugly grid of my bedroom window—
the wires were like nerves inside of bones—
and though I grasped that they kept me from harm
I sometimes still felt as if imprisoned,
as if I was the one who'd done something wrong.
A tree stood sentry outside, and for a long
while before sleep, until the moon had risen
and escaped its net of branches, I'd follow.
I didn't know then about the letter
from my mother's ex-husband, its unveiled threats,
that for years would keep her own sleep shallow.
No matter that my room seemed a giant crib—
I was its beating heart, gazing through its ribs.

GOOD EGG

The threading finally shot
on the window crank,

I disassemble the unit
and out falls a tiny egg,

like a porcelain ball bearing.
It may have been there for years.

Which of the parrots
that babble in the gable

left it here
one cool Spring day

before I shut my windows
for months of air conditioning?

The innocent bird delicately
lifting the egg in its beak

and into its little
nest of steel,

like a precious stone
placed in a setting—

the way many will
rest their trust,

while the window is still open,
in a world or in someone

that may or may not deserve it.

Runaway

You'd think I'd done it just last week,
the way my mother still brings up
the time I ran away, at eight
or nine, and stayed unfound for hours.
In a cave of my own making
beneath the bleachers at the park
I hid, nursing some slight now long-
forgotten, and the growing sense
of my own power, watching as
the afternoon slowly darkened,
and the other kids ran off the fields
toward their houses. I stared out
as various vehicles passed;
a patrol car crept by, looking,
probably, for me. It stopped, once,
almost, but kept going. I held
my breath till it turned the corner.
Streetlights were blinking on, the air
cooling, when I made up my mind
that they had been punished enough,
and slipped on home the mile or so
by way of alleys and back yards.
I walked in then as if nothing
had happened, like I'd just come home
from work, and as if my parents
weren't frantic. When their tears had dried
they marched me off with all dispatch
to the police station, where I

stared up at a tall man behind
a tall counter and whispered out
an apology. He must have
heard it, nodding that way, but I
don't think my parents ever did.

CATFISH

He doesn't seem aware of anything,
the little spotted catfish, not the water
sloshing out the goldfish bowl I cradle

in my lap, my hand too small to cap the top.
Not the car my father struggles now to hold
in its lane, not this morning's driving rain,

not my stormy, damaged little brother
in the back seat, who has chosen this moment
to unleash a tantrum pounding his fists

against my father's head and shoulders. No,
he appears as calm as ever, unperturbed,
my sweet-natured favorite, and after five years

the lone survivor of all the other fish,
the flashy tetras, passionate gouramis,
clown loaches. Peaceable, agreeable,

steady and industrious bottom feeder,
whisker-nosed vacuum of sediment, tranquil-
eyed even now. It is time to redo

the living room, my mother says, and with one
fish left, the aquarium has to go.
But I can't just flush him down the drain—

which is why, on the way to my brother's
Small Fry Day Camp, we're stopping at the pet store,
so I can drop off my friend by the door

like a foundling—and then turn to watch, past
my brother's head, through the rear window, the bowl,
as it disappears behind all that rain.

FORTUNE

About her brief, childless, dark first marriage
to a man with a family fortune,
my mother always kept very quiet.
All I knew was that it ended in his threat

to hurl acid in her flawless face, her friends
hustling her out of town early one morning.
No glance back, no contesting the estate.
How she fled to Florida, to start again.

It seemed a long way from the life she shared
for nearly forty years with my father.
And I was long grown when my mother heard
that he had settled just a few miles from us,

the first husband, in retirement, maybe.
But more years passed, my father passed away,
and the ex stayed silent—until one day
word arrived that he too had died, alone,

on a houseboat moored on the Intracoastal,
the body not found for almost a week.
And only then did my mother disclose
other threats made at the time—how he vowed

to track her down (before the Internet,
all you needed was money), and to kill
any children she had. It shadowed her,
over the years, at the mind's edge, waiting,

and she could never have told my brother
and me. Eventually it would have grown
familiar, less insistent, less probable,
if never quite erased. For my mother,

hearing of his death must have been like a rope
loosening, a boat drifting slowly to sea.

BELATED ELEGY

John Buckley (1956-1970)

We made fun of him for nearly everything,
but mostly, I see now, for being poor:
the bad buck teeth his parents couldn't afford
braces for; the one-speed, old-style, heavy Schwinn;
how slow he was in school. But the morning
the principal came on the public address
to say in hushed tones that John had failed to cross
the street in time, the other kids' bikes churning
ahead, it was his parents we thought about:
older than most of our own, in their fifties
by then, he had no brothers or sisters
and we must have known there would be no more.
The first boy like me I knew who'd died. Boy
like me: I'd never seen him that way before.

THE GIFT

It could be straight out of Norman Rockwell:
a boy on a swale, swinging at golf balls
with a 29-inch Louisville Slugger,
for his flag a palm tree, his cup a sprinkler hole.
The title might be, *Taking Up a New Sport.*
The boy is me; he's eight. And in the corner,
just barely visible, is a young man,
twenty maybe, watching from the sidewalk
this small figure's strange improvisations
as he stages entire tournaments
in his head, he's Nicklaus, Palmer, Player,
back and forth and across the quiet street
till the summer evening finally sends him in.

Then Rockwell paints the second in a series:
it's later that night; the sitter answers
the door, where in the porchlight the young man stands
next to a golf bag full of clubs. They're old,
he's explaining, but it's a complete set,
just gathering dust in the garage, in fact
belonged once to a cousin who is now—
here we see the boy appearing from behind
the sitter, eyes widening—because he knows
the touring professional cousin's name,
has seen him on TV. Call this one *The Gift*,
and the child will hardly sleep this night, dreaming
of his future charmed by a first set of clubs.

It's now the next morning, and Rockwell struggles
with this scene: the boy's mother in the car,
outside the young man's house; at the front door
her husband, somber-eyed, her son in tears;
and the young man and his father, confusion,
questioning on their faces. Between them all,
the bag; like a foursome ready to tee off.
In measured tones the boy's father is explaining
how his son has broken a household rule,
simply, and while the child continues to stare
at his shoes, his chin wet, his mother can see
something else, something she cannot stop herself
from seeing, because she is a mother:

a warm afternoon, and dusty sunlight
slants down through the jalousies at the back
of the young man's garage. Neither father
is home yet, but a tour is underway
among old footballs and chess sets and other
items of interest to an eight-year-old.
There are few sounds; some birds, someone distantly
cutting his grass. The young man's hand touches
her son's cheek; the boy's long lashes lower.
Before she can shake herself from this vision,
her child has already begun the long walk
back to the car, sure that his beautiful
future has just been returned and lost for good.

OLD FLORIDA POSTCARD

"careless, corrupt state...the poorest postcard of itself"

— Elizabeth Bishop

Although the two little black boys
are sitting on a limestone wall,

legs dangling, crossed at the ankles,
and barefoot, the caption straddles

no fences: "Florida Natives:
Pickaninnies and Coconuts."

The boys appear to be smiling
(one's overalls ripped and baggy

at the knees), about to sink teeth
into the sweet white meat, the shells

on their laps split open like skulls,
and for once it is something more

than the collector in me glad
this card was never inscribed, or

sealed to send with anyone's stamp.

MY FATHER'S ARSENAL

"Get it out of here!" my mother screamed each time
another weapon turned up—my father,
the gentlest man I knew, whose calling me "sweetheart"
made my girlfriend cringe, had secreted around
the house a stockpile, for my mother's safety

and his own. A pistol beneath the mattress
in the guest bedroom. A switchblade buried deep
inside the nightstand, nightstick under the seat
of his car. That Christmas, the first without him,
we stumbled on a hidden compartment

of the antique rolltop desk, and a small
brown bag of bullets. Each new discovery
itself an invasion, frightening her
almost as much as anything it might have
guarded against. Pawn shop or police station,

someone would take them, she pointed to the door
and I would carry them off in a bag,
like a burglar or crime scene technician.
But I would wait till she turned the deadbolt
behind me, listen as she latched the chain.

EMILY DICKINSON AND THE BOSTON RED SOX

October 27, 2004

In her white cap with the scarlet B
she watches the small color TV

(no flat-screen, plasma, or LCD
for her, she would have you know), and she

much admires the home team's jerseys
and jackets, thinking, what a lovely

bird, the cardinal, at her feeder
that blur of passion, and how lucky

in a way—a strange way—they will be
now, those fans west of here, the trophy

so close… Unlike all those poor Yankee
stalwarts, year after year, their routine

champagne and ticker-tape, how truly
deprived, not knowing what desire means.

In fact she's traveled to the city
only once, when she had that pesky

eye malady and went in to see
specialists at the Infirmary.

But first came the cab ride—her kindly
driver!—straight to Fenway, and the Green

Monster, a name she wishes keenly
she'd coined herself, for Spring, with the trees

out beyond the fences suddenly
looming… And it is only envy

that she feels now, eyeing the melee
on the mound, the grass thinning this deep

in Fall, for all the dumbstruck seated
there, mute, staring at the other team—

her team—leaping deliriously
with their improbable victory,

and all of that sweet joy already
slipping away so naturally.

II

WALKING WITH MY MOTHER

For years with my long strides
I hurried ahead of her into stores,

the bank, supermarket, movie theaters.
By the time she needed a cane

and an arm, I had learned to slow
my pace to hers. She might have leaned

on a walker, or yielded to a wheelchair.
Instead, I became like a father of a bride

handing her off that day with her shy smile
to the dark-suited groom at the end of the aisle.

RECOMMENDATION

Her poem touched me, and it made me laugh,
a sweet and witty elegy for her cat,
and after she graduated I wrote
a long, enthused letter on her behalf
when she applied to join the police force.
Whatever possessed me, later, to Google
her lines, finding she'd lifted them wholesale
from an obscure British poet, my first
thought was to write again—to her sergeant.
But then I stopped; she'd put one over on me,
and I hoped she wasn't patrolling the streets,
assigned anything dangerous or urgent,
but using her true talents at a desk,
investigating fraud, or identity theft.

GOODBYE, APOSTROPHE

Goodbye, apostrophe—
you were barely hanging on

at the top of the line
by one curled fingertip,

and now it appears you've fallen
from the keypads of all the smartest phones—

forgive my possessiveness
toward you.

Goodbye, turn signal—
hiding behind the steering wheel,

whatever indestructible composite
you're made of,

no one in this town
seems to need you anymore—

I don't know which way to go
without you.

Goodbye, incandescent lightbulb—
you took up all my energy

but these sinuous newcomers
lack your warmth,

your hominess—
when the rare idea

comes to me now,
what flashes on above my head?

Goodbye, Mom—
when I went to pick up your ashes today,

a squirrel darted beneath my car—
then came out the other side, unscathed,

as if there weren't room in the world
for one more death, however small...

My light, my direction,
mine—goodbye.

MISSIONARY

Before my next-door neighbor left for Yemen
to bring Christianity to the Muslims,
she bought a gorgeous, snowy Himalayan

because she wanted some companionship
and doubted her old cat would survive the trip.
She hoped to find someone willing to adopt

the fifteen-year-old tabby who'd been with her
through everything, through the bitter divorce,
kids growing up and away, that time her car

burned on the expressway. Behind the screen door
the old cat glared as my tireless neighbor
dragged the upstart in a training halter

around and around the courtyard, the youngster
bug-eyed and gassed from straining at the collar.
And while the stack of boxes grew taller

and my neighbor was learning Arabic,
the aging tabby, who'd endured, arthritic
and asthmatic, for years, suddenly fell sick

with a spreading fungus and was quarantined
in the bathroom. With her house in order—
or at least her apartment in storage—

my neighbor asked if I would take her poor girl
to the vet and put her down: it would "hurt her"
too much. "I'll go *with* you," I said—not the words

she wanted to hear. Next day, one last hello
at my door. "I'm off to the land of Allah!"
she said. "Wish me luck. And God keep you always."

MY FAVORITE NUMBER

When I was a boy, my mother liked to ask

my favorite number—no matter that she knew
the answer. "Twulve!" I'd exclaim, mispronouncing,

which no doubt added to her amusement.

Even when I was grown, she still inquired,
and I could always make her smile, saying

the word the way I did as a child.

When she died on the 12th, had she known the date—
all track lost by then of the hours, months, the year,

of almost everything except for who I was—

I think she would have laughed, then apologized,
then laughed, as I try to now, for her sake.

CLASS PHOTO: TOMBSTONE, ARIZONA, 1892

So that no boy's hand
tugs a girl's hair
or wanders to his nose,
the photographer has had
all forty or so pose
with arms folded frankly
across their chests—
the picture taken
in front of their one-room
schoolhouse, all dressed
in their best knee-length
suits and dusty,
laced-up boots.
They range in age
from maybe six
to sixteen, but only one
or two have allowed themselves—
or gotten away with—
a smile. Their teachers,
the two women at the back
in high, white starched shirts
are the only ones
whose arms aren't crossed.
But their pupils stare past
the man, black-hooded
like an executioner,
in what they've accepted

as the posture in which
one meets eternity—
especially those
who have seen their fathers
similarly arranged,
but framed
in a long pine box,
their eyes forever closed
just as the flash went off.

THE LITTLE BLUE PURSE

It was a little blue purse she had asked for,
my mother, age four, when her father called

from the Mayo Clinic. With a silver chain—
and he had somehow found one in a pawnshop

in Rochester, and if he weren't so tired—
from the radium and the transfusions,

from the talk of white blood cells, from the drive
itself—then he might have noticed sooner

that he'd left the purse at a small motel
near the Canadian border. And so,

with his family waiting for him, wife
and three daughters, my mother the youngest,

at the lake at Winnipeg Beach that summer,
he turned back, though it would mean many more hours…

She was kept, my mother, from his funeral,
and her own mother allowed no photograph

of him in the house—but my mother kept
the little blue purse, in a trunk she carried

into adulthood, with books and letters
and clothes from her early years. And the trunk,

too big for my parents' first apartment,
was stored at my father's plant, where someone

stole it—and the only thing my mother said
she missed was the little blue purse. Almost all

of which had slipped from my mind, out walking
on the afternoon of her death, her body

bagged and crematorium-bound just hours
before, and I had gone a hundred yards more

before realizing what I had just passed,
sitting on a limestone wall at eye-level—

a purse, that someone had discarded or lost,
for all the world a child's purse, cheap, plastic,

and a light blue. When we were kids we would swear
on our mothers' lives—what do I swear on now?—

but when I came around again, the purse
was gone, the sky just turning from clear to dusk.

INSTINCT

The wasp that stung
your pretty lip
that time you strayed
too near its nest,
merely obeyed
its instinct—

much the way
I find my mouth
moving toward yours
whenever you allow
yourself to slip
within my vicinity.

MOTHER AND SON

My mother always looked so youthful, so late
in life, that out at dinner sometimes waiters
would mistake us for husband and wife. She'd laugh.
But I still wasn't prepared to learn, after
receiving by mail her birth certificate
(just weeks before her death certificate),
sent away for because of discrepancies
in Medicare and Social Security—
that she was actually five years older
than I'd always known her to be. She'd altered
the date, it seems, early in adulthood...
but why? "So many things I never told you,"
she told me, one night we thought would be her last.
I held her hand, waited; watched; the moment passed.

Body and Blood

With all the rising and sitting and kneeling
and sitting and rising in the hard pews
of the poorly-ventilated All-Saints

Episcopal Church, no wonder your low
blood pressure had you dizzy and weak so
that the next thing you knew you were fainting

and the ushers dragged you by the armpits
out the pulpit door to revive you, fanning
your ghostly face with the morning program,

your mother in their wake up the aisle—*Honey,
are you all right?*—peering above you, pressing
to your damp forehead the back of her hand.

A century before and you'd be deemed
a special blessed case, redeemed by the Lord
to heed His calling—who could not hear His Word

in church without eyes rolling back and swooning,
and your mother soon would have seen you secured
in a convent, all days to come, as a ward

of Christ Himself, even the oldest lifers
whispering of your devotion. But you'd wonder,
jolting upright on your unforgiving cot

some mornings, why the sudden lightheadedness—
until it came back, remembering how the Lord
had stayed by your side all of the night, cotton

murmur at your ear, His hand warm on your brow.

FATHER AND SON

By the time my brother reached his twenties,
my father, concerned he had never had sex

or ever would—disabled that he was,
especially socially—considered

recruiting a prostitute, someone kind,
discreet, and which friend or acquaintance to ask

to set it in motion. In the old days
he might have just taken Rob to a brothel,

waiting on an overstuffed, pillowed divan
for however long that first time required,

the other ladies eyeing my handsome,
happily married father, him nodding

politely back. After a while out
would my brother have tottered, a bit unkempt,

shy half-smile, leading by the hand the girl,
who tousles his hair and looks up knowingly

at my father, who mouths his thanks, and puts
his arm around my brother, who so far

as I know has never been with a woman,
and is nearly the age my father was then.

LOWER 9TH WARD

All those years our heights
penciled on the porch's doorframe—
now our lives forever
measured by a single line
left above

DEAD RICK

Ten months later, my brother still can't believe
Rick's dead. "His car's still at his building!"
Rick once bummed some money off my brother,
a hundred bucks, and never paid it back.
Won't now either, I point out. He also crashed
a lot on my brother's couch, especially
near the end. "That's all he did, chain-smoke and sleep!"

My brother always carries wads of cash.
Years ago, my father, about to drop
my brother's jeans in a washing machine,
found in the pockets 90 dollars in bleached,
crumbling bills. He shook out other things as well,
stones, hamburger wrappers, bottlecaps, the stuff
my brother always picks up off the street.

Rick was 52. At least he would drive
my brother places, the five miles to work
sometimes, as Rob's never gotten his license.
But you have to wonder. "Bob!" he'd shout and cough.
(No one calls my brother anything but Rob
or Robert.) "Where are we, man? I don't know
this part of town, and have you seen my glasses?"

With my father in the passenger seat,
my brother, still in his teens then, slowly steered
the Chevrolet around the neighborhood,
but he never went in to take the test.

Now, at 42, he rides a mountain bike
up the hills of New Haven to his job
wrangling the outsize carts at a Sam's Club.

Between Sam's and Uncle Sam—his benefits
from the government—my brother has enough
to help out anyone who asks. Plenty do.
Goodness knows he spends virtually nothing
on himself. But he can't let go the fact
that Rick is gone. Every few weeks or so
he bikes the couple miles to Rick's apartment,

and peers inside the '95 Taurus
as if he expected his friend to pop up,
from the back seat maybe, rub his sleepy eyes
and light another cigarette. Rick left
an aging mother somewhere in Florida,
and supposedly a sister lives not far.
Someone will fetch his car, I tell my brother,

but truthfully I could see it slowly
rusting, winter after winter, until
the building's owner finally has it towed.
As long as it's there, though, for my brother
it's as if Rick really might be showing up
any time now, knocking on his door, saying,
"Bob, man! I've got a check coming. Just let me…"

To His Coil Mattress

Intimate of one-third my life
(who, after all, closer than you?),
for your decade's faithful duty
you've earned more than my gratitude,
you have my commiseration,
as surely I've been no blessing
to put up with, or just put up,
with all those turnings and tossings—
how you suffered my many moods,
the haphazard hours I kept,
the nights I lay awake with doubts
when others would have simply slept.
I am thankful for your patience,
your resilience: every few months
I could literally flip your world
upside down and around, not once
did you voice a note of complaint.
For both our sakes I would have liked
to have given your springs and coils
more frequent, vigorous workouts,
the sort of pleasurable toil
you were made for, but then again,
who ever admits to enough?
You had my back (my side, my front)
when the absences could be tough.
Still, it was inevitable:
with me weighing on you, each night
for all those years, that you'd become,

in time, depressed—how could you not?
And to say I went to the mat,
threw myself prostrate at dozens
to find a replacement worthy,
I know it shouldn't, and doesn't,
mean a thing to you. You needed,
finally, to move on. Tomorrow,
then, when your successor arrives,
you will depart not in sorrow
but celebrating what you've meant:
O launching pad of all my dreams,
O cushioned float from dark to light—
buoying me past what lay between—
on this, our last night together,
wherever bound when you leave me,
I wish you a sleep as peaceful
as you gave your life to give me.

INTIMACIES

It could only block sight,
that plasterboard wall between
the converted bedrooms. All winter
in that Iowa basement,
Matt and his friend David
braided their voices to the furrows
of their bodies, while I lay
a carpenter's shortcut away,
layered in sweaters,
trying to read through
the bedsprings' creak
and feeling the floor we shared shake.

But one night climbing
the cellar steps, I surprised them
there in the warm, dark kitchen,
hands hooked into each other's jeans
in the gentlest of embraces.
Embarrassed, they both turned
to face me, letting go of their broken
clinch, but I was already
out through the coatroom,
and out of the house,
putting a wall between us,
as if it were necessary.

ACADEMIC DISCOURSE IN WESTERN MASSACHUSETTS

Amherst, 1979

When a homely wooden cross was set afire
one night on the lawn of the black students' house,
the campus was stunned—this wasn't the South,

after all, but a liberal college town
in the East, and it was almost the eighties.
You wore white sheets to frathouse toga parties.

Two hours away raged the gang wars of Boston,
but you wondered: *Here?* Could the locals harbor
such hatred, were supremacists everywhere?

A college-wide meeting was quickly called,
and we all gathered on the floor of the gym,
students, faculty, administration,

hundreds of us crosslegged like yogis,
people standing to make their points. Some shouted.
Some wept. All spoke passionately, sincerely.

It was agreed that we did not discuss
these matters nearly enough, that these ancient
antagonisms simmered among us,

in our classrooms, cafeteria, the quad.
We vowed that something positive would rise
from this horror, but a few days later,

when the two-by-fours were traced to the basement
of the black house, their leaders stepped forward
and confessed that yes, they had lashed the beams

and poured the gasoline and struck the match.
And for a second time we were thrown into shock
and grief. But hadn't it accomplished, they asked,

just what they'd intended? Weren't we all talking,
for once, thrashing out our deep divisions?
Wasn't it justified, by whatever means?

And finally the College answered—rightly—*No*.
There could be no saving explanation,
no reason. Just weeks from graduation,

the perpetrators were expelled, and we thought
the matter closed. Frisbees sailed through the quad
again, speakers blared from open windows.

We were busy making summer plans. And then
the copycats began—across the county,
one after another, crosses searing

the night sky, and now we had our answer: *Here?*
And this time we knew the color of their skin.
It was as if they had been given a license,

been waiting for just the opportunity,
and they had not the slightest interest
in dialogue, in negotiation…

No one was ever caught. They slinked away
into the night, into the past, into
the future. Half-hidden, biding their time.

By the warm afternoon in May when we cleared
out our rooms, the burnings had subsided,
like the whitened coals in a grill, and the gym,

since we wouldn't be needing it that summer,
echoed now with the sounds of local kids,
divided evenly into shirts and skins.

III

HISTORY

On a walking tour of historic homes
in my old neighborhood, we enter a house
that slowly dawns on me as belonging
to the family of a girl I knew
in junior high—good-looking, intelligent,

vivacious and popular—and who died
suddenly, not much after, in college,
of a heart condition never diagnosed.
She was editor of our ninth grade yearbook,
so it's no surprise she's everywhere in it,

and in my copy she signed each photo,
crossing out in one her face and writing,
"I hate this picture!" That year she dated
a black classmate, when at the time not one
black family lived anywhere in our town.

And now I am walking through her old house,
which I had never visited back then,
just a boy from school, and into her bedroom,
which her parents have evidently left
as she might have last seen it, the lone twin bed,

the Frampton posters, cramped desk, box turntable.
Our guide is pointing something out, but I'm
not listening, for just now I am closer
to her than I ever was, and am learning
another kind of history of this house.

Downstairs again, I introduce myself
to her mother, who has been patiently
waiting with a pitcher of lemonade
for us to file through. She smiles, and claims
to remember my name. Next to the door

hangs a large family photo, with Beth
standing front and center, her gaze directed
just above the camera, taken likely
not long before she died. I pause there briefly,
and we resume our leisurely tour, as our

guide draws a line across his list of houses.

TYPING CLASS WITH MRS. A.

Archbishop Curley High School

To stop us looking at our hands,
still used to hunting and pecking,
Mrs. Altman always brandished
a pool cue, whacking our knuckles

or temples when regrettably
we glanced down. She liked to lean in
over shoulders, especially
boys'—she hadn't been keen on

coeducation—and was known
to sometimes drape one enormous
breast on each side of a young man's
neck; and routinely alarmed us

by showing at our favorite beach
in an ill-fitting bikini.
Yet to insist that her teaching
made little impression on me

(apart from my formative skull)
would not be at all accurate,
for while I've never had the skill
to type 60 words a minute,

still my fingers can find their way
around a keyboard (and I don't
look down!), and even to this day
I recite to my own students

her line, "When in doubt, put them out"—
quotation marks, and how they flank
commas and periods (and how
we misuse them!). At least I think

it's what she meant, when she, bending
over me, in a throaty voice
to ensure my comprehending,
spoke those words in a low-cut blouse.

TYPOS

I urge my students to watch for typos:
how do I know that you mean *tap* dancer
when I'm staring hard at a *lap* dancer?
And your performing unasked-for *lipo*
on the great and ancient Chinese poet
is unintentional, I'm sure, but lacks
respect, all the same. *Pubic* goes *public*
too often these days—to what do we owe it?—
loins are *lions* when the mood's conducive,
and *immoral*, yes, has proved *immortal*
since probably time immemorial,
but your paper's not the place to prove it.
Did old poets write with rhyme and *meaner*?
Or with a more cheerful *misdemeanor*?

3RD PERIOD MATH: MR. D.

His was the one class you arrived
early for, but not for a seat
up front: Mr. Donahue,
a chain-smoker with yellow teeth,

was a lisper and a spitter,
and could manage, on a good day,
trajectories of several feet.
"Ith juth math, kidsth!" he'd stop and say,

from a cloud of chalk at the board,
from which rain would routinely fall.
On breaks he'd rush to a closet
housing science lab chemicals

and light up—or fill up, it seemed.
He lived in a lean neighborhood
near the Pussycat Theatre
and adult bookstores, where cars slowed

for men and boys—you do the math.
Whose company after hours
he kept, though, we couldn't care less,
too intent on torment in ours—

spitballs would return the favor,
paper planes ever flattening
against the board, and one morning
when the waterworks were jetting

with particular force, volume
only rarely seen, Paul Mosheim
(nice Jewish boy at a Catholic
school), tardy only that one time,

finally, exasperated,
picked up his textbook and held it,
open, there in the damp front row,
above him like an umbrella.

"Goddamnith!" Donahue thundered,
and swatted the textbook away,
then turned right back to his figures,
as if it happened every day.

My Father on the Tennis Court

"Do not let me hear/Of the wisdom of old men, but
rather of their folly."

— T.S. Eliot

A basket of balls, a net
between us—like twenty-eight

years ago. Only it's me
pitching underhand, slowly,

as near to him as I can.
Him standing uncertain, lock-

kneed, but eager. Sixteen months,
we've waited for just this day:

to tell ourselves, *This is it,*
or *There still might be a chance,*

the tumor partly shrunken,
his feet enough unswollen

to squeeze into stiff Nike's.
Now his first strokes, thick with rust.

The old form's gone. What I thought
would come back quickly, doesn't,

as if he's forgotten all
he taught me. He looks, of course,

pretty damned good: the new shirt
my mother bought, plucky grin—

good as since the MRI,
the smudge like a mark on clay.

He's even had me stop at
Mike's, to swing the latest frames

in the magazines. Always
embracing the new: the first

at the courts to trade his wood
for steel (getting me one too).

Three times he's let his doctors
drill screws through his skull, to fix

tight a gleaming helmet, a
Virtual Reality/

Star Wars contraption firing
cobalt two hundred angles

at the cancer. And more balls
now are coming back, faster,

and just weeks ago I knifed
a smile in two tennis balls

to make wheels for his walker,
so now I toss one wider,

stretching him—only to watch,
surreal slo-mo, bloated feet

crossing him up, my father
going down: Duchamp's *Nude,* piece

by broken piece, or soft-shoe
vaudevillian as the big cane

yanks him offstage. Before I
can reach him, his head hangs there,

a moment, suspended—then
smacks the cement. Toweling

the blood and we could be kids,
conspiring from Mom: if I

can get him to the shower...
But that night, the purple bruise

on his forehead (precisely
where the tumor is staging

its latest rally), and hand,
fractured, swelling, give us up.

Two months he'll wear a cast; three,
he'll be dead. And did my fear

put him on that court? Did he
consent for my sake? *When you*

were a boy, he says, *you asked
to play; I never forced you.*

*Well, it's just like then. Next time,
I think I'll try that graphite…*

THE PRIESTS OF MY ADOLESCENCE

When I see on the news some damaged guy
my age, and across the courtroom the priest,
white-haired and impassive, unrepentant,
I think back to high school, and the Jesuits
who guided my own spurt from boy to man:

studious Father R, who explained to me,
non-Catholic that I was, exactly how Christ
was killed by the Crucifixion, the slow
agony of the asphyxiation;
and jovial Father T, portly and bald,

who'd boxed in his youth and called everyone "Champ"
(at least the boys—I don't know what he called
the girls). And our young principal, Father E,
whom my mother may have had the slightest
crush on, remarking that he was good-looking.

He also had a habit of appearing
in our locker room, just as we'd come in
sweaty from the playing fields and peeling off
our shorts to shower. I don't think he was there
to deliver some rousing, Gipper-like speech

of inspiration; he'd just mill about
in a corner, arms crossed in front of his chest,
maybe saying something to the coaches,
while we moved quickly under the nozzles
and refrained from our usual snapping

of the thin white towels. By the time we were dressed
he had vanished, perhaps to reappear
an hour later for the freshmen. Sometimes
one of us was summoned to his office
for a punishment. The guilty party

would emerge some time thereafter, red-faced
and never wanting to talk about it.
Just last year, I saw where old Father E,
now long-reassigned to another school,
had abruptly resigned from the priesthood—

citing illness—just as the prosecutors
were closing in. Young men had come forward…
And aside from the usual thoughts of
"There but for the Grace…" I wondered about
all the mouths over the years that had opened

in acceptance, unsuspecting, of the host
he dropped—or if those faithful wondered too,
if they ever saw in his sky-blue eyes
what he must have seen himself, just as the steam
was clearing from our locker room mirrors,

before he passed back into the blinding sun.

LONELY HEARTS

Back when they were still speaking to my father,
his two sons from his first marriage brought over
one day their bright new copy of *Sgt. Pepper,*

hoping to turn my father and mother on
to Lucy in the Sky and Mr. Kite.
I was eight, three years from my first 45,

but even I could see the futility
in their trying to bridge, as it was called then,
the Generation Gap—however timeless

the music. With college student earnestness
they persevered, my half-brothers, even
setting up the small box record player

they'd also brought, as if my parents' old four-
legged console stereo were suitable
only for Sinatra and Nat King Cole.

But at least they tried, back then, on holidays
from school they still came over, still would call
my father and sometimes my mother too.

In those days, they thought of her as pretty
and smart and a good cook, which their own mother
would not have wanted to hear. Had they been pressed,

they'd have to admit my father was happy.
But in time—and you would think it might work
the other way—it became harder for them

to forgive, to stop blaming my—our—father
for the divorce. Even into their forties,
feet propped all those years on analysts' couches,

they never made peace with it, could never
understand. By then they were older than
my father had been when he'd filed the papers,

and each was recently divorced himself—
which, who knows, they may have also blamed on him.
So by the time his business, finally,

went under, and then the cancer, they were all
but gone from his life. Each certain, in the way
only a child can be, of his own version

of experience—as if hearing only
what would play on the little turntables
of their hearts, now folded and locked away.

PUNISHMENT

(Fifth Period English: Mrs. Chauveron)

Long gone is whatever we did or said
to merit our punishment, our tenth grade
English class, but it must have been extreme
to provoke our young teacher, whom we esteemed
—no, *loved*... Nor did I recall that our sentence
was the writing of sentences: penance
by essay. I can just hear the grousing
of my peers, our ostentatious fussing
with pens, paper. No memory of what I wrote,
of course, though it seems I included a note,
submitted, no doubt, in peeved disgruntlement,
that *writing should never be a punishment—*
which my teacher, retiring, four decades on,
emails to say she's never forgotten.

THE CONDOM IN MY WALLET

I carried it for years before I lost
(as we knowingly said then) the Big V,
like the coin of a country I wondered
if I would ever visit. I think it cost

a quarter, from one of those gas station
or junior high school boys room vending machines—
the male counterpart to the tampon—though
if anything, it only increased the flow

of blood through my veins, a promise, commitment
waiting to be kept. And in class, sitting
at that metal desk, I seemed to feel it
pulsing upward through my underwear and pants,

so exquisitely tuned was my backside
to its presence. It was there in the first place,
tucked discreetly behind the learner's permit
and cherished bubblegum cartoon, "just in case,"

as some guy had told me I might need it,
as he had heard from another, and so on,
an endless chain of raging testosterone-
driven prudence, experience, wisdom.

And in just what sort of emergency,
I'd ask myself, would it come in handy:
a stuck elevator, a fair young maiden
trapped in the dimming, air-starved shaft with me,

and succumbing to claustrophobia
until I can save her by valiantly
offering the distraction of pleasure…
Did girls lug sponges, diaphragms, IUD's

in that portable pharmacy called a purse?
It wouldn't have mattered. The man prepared
was the fortunate man, we had learned in Scouts.
But looking back, the condom seemed more curse

than talisman, languishing as the wallet
slowly crumbled around it. Finally one night
its moment arrived, but when I pulled it
out, lubricated badly to begin with,

the thing had ossified to nearly stone—
when I stretched it in my hands it shredded,
and the girl just looked at me and shook her head.
Preventer of pregnancy and disease,

it had now prevented sex altogether,
a newly discovered form of abstinence.
O thin repository of so much hope,
the imprint left in imitation leather

sized it up: like a zero on a scorecard,
batter out on strikes, ball still in the yard.

EMERITUS

Craggy, white-haired, venerable, a tower
in his field, we knew, regardless how small
at the podium in the vast lecture hall
he seemed, how frail. Three days a week for an hour
he stood, expounding constitutional law,
no less than the bedrock of our republic.
But I was a freshman, with other subjects
on my mind, and so slept in, missed a slew
of classes, failed to keep up with the readings,
in short blew off the course everyone had urged
I take. And when he died, just on the verge
of the final exam, the College conceding
the entire class an A, he'd given me more
than his life's work, while I made plans for summer.

THE FALL

I could forget, in time, how a half-minute
sooner and I might be running in the rain
across the parking lot, catching his shoulders;
harder to banish is the terror, seen
through wipers, on his face just as he lost
his footing, right before head struck pavement;
and least likely to ever be erased
are his eyes, fixed and staring at the sky,
lips barely moving—breath steady but shallow—
as if tasting for the first time, or last,
the rain. Twelve minutes I knelt, my hand pressed
to his (his walker still clutched), then flashing lights…
Tattooed on his chest: *Do Not Resuscitate*
—words that forever now would come too late.

First Art Lessons

From a book on children's art
you've determined your daughter's
ahead of schedule: at two-
and-a-half already
she's distanced the yardstick
of the stick figure,
and begun adding
eyes and mouth. It's cause
for optimism, if not outright
celebration: she's smart,
and you can take some credit
for that. But if sometimes
she still feels inclined
to indulge in whirls
of expressionist circles
and splotches for the sheer
joy of it—don't be
too quick to see precocity
prodded to prodigy.
Too soon she'll see into
that other anatomy,
the protective layers
we put on to keep
each other out, ourselves
in. My wish is that she stay
a little girl
as long as necessary;
she'll have plenty of time

to master the rudiments,
those tricks
of illusion we learn
that turn the human
from brittle sticks
to solid flesh.

TRADING QINTARS FOR QIVIUTS IN QATAR

Your mother was slot by slot going through
your father's wallet at the intake desk,
searching for his insurance card; while, rooms
away, electrodes sprouted from his chest
and his pulse struggled to locate its rhythm.
Just then a small, folded piece of paper
slipped from one of those compartments hidden
where men conceal notes from their paramours—
but in some strange code: only words beginning
with "q," for which no "u" need follow... *The sneak!*
—a cribsheet he used to beat her at Scrabble!
Next time... But what were his chances of winning,
with his current opponent flush on a streak,
hoarding letters, word score about to triple?

Mistaken

You would remember forever anyway
a kid who'd call, whenever he'd see you,

clear across the crowded campus parking lot
at the end of a long day, and loud enough

for anyone within earshot to hear,
"Best literature professor I ever had!"

And while you would be the first to admit
that his sample size was probably small,

how could you not love a kid like Alvin?
Sometimes you wouldn't even see his face,

just hear his voice from behind a row of cars,
and yet you'd smile, and shake your head, and wave.

And how many times in the years since then
have you driven past the two-story building

where Alvin and his twin brother Alex
kept an office for their fledgling business,

where Alvin studied till late for law school?
Think how often they must have been mistaken

for each other! But the graveyard shift that night,
ever since someone had jimmied the lock,

was Alvin's. And the noise he heard about four
a.m.? A policeman, a few years older,

who'd seen a light on the second floor, and climbed
the stairs—neither knowing that the other

was supposed to be there. It might have mattered
that Alvin had brought a gun for protection—

or not—but one last time, in that dark hallway,
he was mistaken for somebody else…

And all you could do when they buried him
on his—and Alex's—24th birthday,

was to send the family a note and hope—
that he was right, and that you hadn't wasted

very much of what time he had been given.

PAWNBROKER'S WIDOW

Winnipeg, 1938

Neighbor merchants gathered outside their stores
when the officers led her off in cuffs,
my grandmother, to the open back door

of the big black car, like the one she rode
to her husband's burial four years before,
who'd fled with her the pogroms, 41, dead

of leukemia. He'd left her to manage
alone three daughters, and as if betrayed
she'd wiped all trace of him from the house, banished

so much as a photograph. She forbade
the girls from the shop now hers in trade—cameras,
saxophones, brooches, golf bags—and she paid

scant notice to the list the cops dropped off
each week of local items swiped: she could read
no English, though she could speak it well enough,

if accented, "not yet" too much yet like "nyet."
Through iron bars the rabbi offered a stiff
pale hand—ignored—and the lawyer did not

stay long. It was only when a friend appeared
just shy of bail, that words came, not quietly
but language the men would never know or hear,

What can they tell me of stolen things? By now
night had fallen, the children sent home early
from school, waiting for her… Another hour,

her jailers, jangling their keys, with a warning
let her off. Nodding, she said nothing, knowing
exactly how much such caution was worth.

BLOCKAGE

When the CT scan revealed
the artery fully sealed,
the image also disclosed
my body had interposed,
creating new blood vessels
to circumvent the bottle-
neck—a natural bypass
till a stent solved the impasse—
my heart sparing me the knife's
plunge. It may have saved my life.

When the words won't come, when scenes
fail to appear, or to mean
in some signifying way—
an emotional X-ray—
I need to summon the faith
that language will find a path
past any restraint—river
forging an oxbow, diver
dodging bubbles in his lungs—
let speech return to my tongue,

let me live to write again.

ACKNOWLEDGEMENTS

Amoskeag, "My Father on the Tennis Court"

Baseball Bard, "Emily Dickinson and the Boston Red Sox"

Bryant Literary Review, "Goodbye, Apostrophe," "The Fall"

The Carrell, "Old Florida Postcard"

Cloudbank, "The Sprinter"

The Common, "The Little Blue Purse"

Common Ground Review, "To His Coil Mattress"

Connecticut River Review, "Catfish"

The Hopkins Review, "Belated Elegy," "The Condom in My Wallet," "Mistaken," "3rd Period Math: Mr. D.," "Typing Class with Mrs. A."

The Hudson Review, "Warts and All"

J Journal, "Academic Discourse in Western Massachusetts"

Key West Review, "Intimacies"

Magnolia, "Class Photo: Tombstone, Arizona, 1892," "Dead Rick," "Fat Kid," "The Gift," "Lonely Hearts," "The Priests of My Adolescence," "Runaway"

Medical Literary Messenger, "Body and Blood," "Trading Qintars for Qiviuts in Qatar"

Miramar, "History," "Missionary," "My Favorite Number"

New Ohio Review, "The Skeleton in My Grandfather's Closet"

Passages North, "First Art Lessons"

The Raintown Review, "Punishment"

Salamander, "Good Egg"

Southern Poetry Review, "Walking with My Mother"

South Florida Poetry Journal, "Fortune," "Typos"
Spillway, "Lower 9th Ward"
Spoon River Poetry Review, "My Father's Arsenal," "The Ride Home"
Tampa Review, "Boyhood: The Burglar Alarm"
Thought & Action, "Recommendation"
Tigertail, "The Hands"

"Fat Kid" appeared in the anthology, *Changing Harm to Harmony* (Bullies & Bystanders), Joseph Zaccardi, ed.

"Instinct" was a winner of the Porter-Fleming Literary Competition, Morris Museum of Art, Augusta, GA.

Special thanks to Jeffrey Harrison, Walter Lew, Anne Hickok Miller, and Susan Beckham Zurenda, whose close and careful reading of these poems improved this collection in all kinds of ways.

A few of these poems bear specific dedications:

"Class Photo: Tombstone, Arizona, 1892," to Frank Early

"Body and Blood," and "Trading Qintars for Qiviuts in Qatar," to Anne Hickok Miller

"Punishment," to Dorothy Devorah Sklaroff

"3rd Period Math: Mr. D.," and "Typing Class with Mrs. A.," to Susan Beckham Zurenda